Handling the Bones

Also by J. David Cummings

Tancho

Handling the Bones

~

J. David Cummings

Poems

Broadstone

Library of Congress Control Number 2022946066

ISBN 978-1-956782-27-1

Text & Cover Design by Larry W. Moore

Broadstone Books
An Imprint of
Broadstone Media LLC
418 Ann Street
Frankfort, KY 40601-1929
BroadstoneBooks.com

For my children, Kim and Michael, and my wife, Chris

Contents

III. THIS MIND THAT THINKS AND THINKS IT IS NOT DUST

IV. A FEW REMARKS IN PASSING—*JISEI* POEMS

Introduction

In this collection of unsparing, well-crafted poems, David Cummings tells us what he knows of the love affair between his mother and his glamorous, self-destructive father. He was its consequence, born a "jaundiced little yellow albatross," living proof of his mother's shame in a time when they made you pay for unlicensed passion.

The beginning poem evokes the oppressive atmosphere of the blue collar neighborhood where he grew up. People were …*eager to snicker and shame / the daughter back from college, / her family, the baby boy.* When, as a child playing too near a neighbor's door, a man came out and hurled a word at him he didn't understand, his furious mother stormed over and stood outside yelling through the door. *She'd have killed that s.o.b.*

The weight of that judgement was heavy and the vacuum left by his father's absence hard to bear. In a beautifully observed poem "The Runaway," the seven-year-old runs away from his mother, who goes after him. They're on opposite sides of the street, she trying to coax him home, he refusing, wetting himself, crying, and finally, giving in. She asks him why. The poet of his future replies: *I know the boy cannot answer.*

A year later, his father, Jack, dies of drink and desolation. He had met him only once, when he was four: a stranger in uniform sitting on the couch, his mother saying, "David, this is your father." Overwhelmed and speechless, he goes to his room. *But haven't I dreamed dreams in which I…said I was good / at hide-and-seek? And haven't you said / you were good at it too?*

His mother and his relatives made up stories about his father to try to sweeten the bitterness. He believed them until he didn't. But he found the hidden cache of letters Jack had sent to his mother, and would take them from their hiding place in a desk drawer to read, loving the life and poetry he found in them; carefully putting them back.

Meanwhile, his mother struggled against the forces holding her down. She loved art, maybe had lovers on her occasional weekends alone, but hid herself from him. In an astonishing poem "Monday, September 27" the poet imagines the day of his own birth, and then the day of Jack's death, when she (and somehow, it's so well imagined—he, the poet) must give birth to sorrow and rage.

The shadow of Jack was dark over his son's life for many years. *It's not as if / I haven't lived / my own version / of your misspent life* he tells his dead father. He goes off to college, but makes a mess of it, sleeping days, chasing women, marrying too young, divorcing ten years later, drinking. He and his mother become estranged, then gradually, they reconnect. She dies of cancer in middle age, chain smoking to the end, her son at her side.

This wonderfully rich book has room for much more than sorrow and regret. The poet begins to come to terms with abundant life and its redemptions, its loves. "American Rootless" shows him at his mother's grave near Valley Forge on a winter day, the *sky the slate-gray / of sullen February*. He gives himself up to the storm: *to the hard memories it demanded. Sorrow got a hold. For a while, / I held my ground.*

Things start to turn around. He finds a new love, a remarkable woman, a poet whose sorrow finds an echo in his and whose sense of life inspires him. *I call her the summer of my mind*, he writes.

In a triumphant poem "Praise Dust" a great vision of the world takes shape and seems to burst out of the poet into an ecstatic litany of homage: *Praise this mind that thinks / And thinks it is not dust, / Praise us, soul-demented beings of ruin, / Praise chance, praise words, praise love, / And praise the dust swirling the field this very moment.*

And finally, among the meditations of the book's last section, the *Jisei* Poems, there's a "Sonnet for a Small Forgotten Child" in which the poet looks back. His life is happy now, but he has a strange unease, *as if something were still undone / as if a small forgotten child / …were calling to me across the dust of eighty years. / I know him, know his injury, / …how it found its way to poems / he never imagined writing, / his soul the melancholy there / …but there's no time in which he knows / the words.* In the end he brings together the man he is and the boy he was with four words of earned wisdom: *Such a hard equation.*

—Charlotte Muse

But who can hope his lines should long
Last in a daily changing tongue…
We write in sand, our language grows,
And like the tide our work o'erflows.
—Edmund Waller

he said the great presence
that permitted everything and transmuted it
in poetry was passion
passion was genius…
—W. S. Merwin

HANDLING THE BONES

A near-the-end man is entering his bones.
You can sense the stopping-hour come into the room,
the sacrament of the body as it quiets,
the gathering grief, the half-welcomed mercy.

≈

Or it might be a seasoned collector of bones
has stopped by a roadside outcrop to examine
the steep hillside cut: exposed, unstable layers
where the asphalt road pitches sharply down and left.

≈

Why have we stopped, half-invited? Why watch
as he scrapes the rock face, freeing fossils—
each loosened bone's inevitable fall,
the sacred heft? How to take the measure?

≈

The matriarch's long dead. Still, the gray troupe
of elephants is stopping at the sight,
encircling her. They are handling the bones.
What's it meant to mean
if not but to remember that great heart?

I. Requiem for Eva Mae & Jack

"All's misalliance,
Yet why not say what happened?"
—Robert Lowell

ALBATROSS

We were blue collar stock,
with blue collar neighbors
eager to snicker and shame
the daughter back from college,
her family, the baby boy.

Lives led inside of lives,
soft turtle flesh and shell—
crack it open,
the life's gone when you get there.

Once she called a neighbor out.
A strange word spat at the boy
playing too near the neighbor's door.
He ran home, scared, asked her
what it meant. She didn't say.
Instead she stormed from the house
and into the street, and stood there,
a thin, raw wire
shouting at a shut door.
She'd have killed that s.o.b.

Fragments of an Afternoon

You were sitting on the sofa…

if I remember it—

by yourself…

leaning forward, forearms
resting on your thighs…

in uniform…

beige cap folded in your hands—

Above me, my mother, saying
"David, this is your father,"

myself half-hidden
behind her skirt, her voice
the calming waters—

was I four?

How had you gotten there,
you who had been nowhere I knew of?

Minutes refused to pass…

Without words? Without touch?

I went to my room.

But haven't I dreamed dreams
in which I crossed to you,
stuck out my hand
for you to shake,

said I was good
at hide-and-seek?

And haven't you said
you were good at it too?—

A seashore, ·
a child spading holes
in wet sand, watching the ocean
fill in each vacancy

till every trace of you is water.

And yet a young man

is sitting on a worn sofa,
his innocence
a small imprisoned light

as lost in the roil of his life
as are the two

who will live
all the years of his death.

THE RUNAWAY

The woman is twenty-eight or nine
and skinny. She is chasing a young boy,
maybe seven—or rather, she is trying
to catch him; for he is running away from home.
It's an odd moment, a Saturday,
a warm drizzle that morning, the afternoon
overcast and damp and close. It's July in
eastern Pennsylvania, the war's still on,
and it's time for the boy to come in from play.
No doubt it started innocently enough,
a child's game of chase, a small rebellion,
but a melancholy has come into it.
You can tell she senses it. Her laugh's edgy,
a whine has crept into her pleas, and the boy,
who has stopped running, is beginning to cry.
He has peed his pants, and for what seems a long time
there's this little standoff, the mother
on one side of the narrow street, the child
directly across. She says the boy's name,
a brief quiet, "come on, let's go home,"
calmly as she can, but you can hear the grief.
The boy can say nothing; he stands frozen
except for the sobs that shake him. He is
entirely unknown to himself, and frightened.
—Then it's over. He crosses to his mother,
they turn up the street and walk slowly side by side.
She asks, why? I know the boy cannot answer.

Visiting Jack, the Letters

Myself ten years old, maybe twelve,
pulling out the packet of letters again,
untying the green ribbon, no one
to see I had stolen into her desk
again, the bottom drawer, where they lived
their shadow life, half-hidden
under some important looking papers.

They were there maybe a dozen years,
although they must have stopped coming
four or five years earlier, your body
by that time well into its moldering
in ground I was yet to visit,
and reading them, how alive your voice,
speaking little things to sweeten her, speaking love.

Eight letters or nine was all there was
to have of you and not often have.
I'd put them back carefully, same order
as I found, and re-tie the ribbon exactly
so it would seem no one had disturbed them,
and I never thought that for her there was
an infinity more of you, which was an infinity

of nothing, and her whole life to get through
and stories to make up for me, and letters
saying things I wouldn't see down into
till I too betrayed a lover with high sounding
words like yours of love and leave-taking,
all the while in another woman's bed,
plying all the while those Irish echoes

of the self-tormented poet rummaging
the shadows of greatness like gossip
running the back fences. And down into
what I came to know of drunken poets

who didn't write poems, only sprawling letters
at midnight, and down into the ruin
of lovers, you and the waiting myth.

~

She taught me how to draw.
Quiet afternoons when
I wasn't running the streets
with the neighborhood kids.
The beginnings of art.
But she never took it
up again or painted.
Sometimes she would steal off
to New York and the art
museums, maybe a
lover in tow, someone
she would never speak of.

We were iron branded
and you the brand, long dead
before I could sort out
the theft: as if *we three*
were sealed in a cheap box,
a rundown Catholic
cemetery, upstate
New York, family plot.
And those keepsake letters,
a true poet's, and me,
crazy to grow up you,
put aside art and her.

~

She must have been out of her mind
in love with you that freshman year,
the two of you free for the last time,
though you would not have known that then.
Then, it was novels and poems
and talk, papers to write for class,
philosophy and art, politics,
late afternoons on the Quad,
accelerating flirtations,
something promised, that first time
and the seeming, overwhelming rightness.
How could you know how wrong it would go?

I say out of her mind in love because
though you left college, left her pregnant,
left your own promise for the darkness in you,
you never left her mind, even after there could be
no more letters back and forth, after
she destroyed them decades later, even at the end,
after they took away the gin martinis,
dried her out for chemo & unpalatable hospice fare,
only her cigarettes left: there you were, among
her last words to me, but still her secret.

THE COED

She liked to read, and she liked smoking cigarettes.
And she loved art and painting and
should have gone to New York to live.
Looking back, her life seems one long failure
and maybe she came to see it that way too, unless
you were to count the men, which is something,
which she kept from me. She had her reasons.
Or maybe exactly because of that, the men.
They were never Jack, never that first illusion.

She wasn't Doris Day pretty but not as homely
as I thought when I was kid. Then girls
had to be cute and bright and women beautiful,
although I wasn't sure what made
a woman beautiful. But a few days ago
I started digging out old photographs
from some banged up boxes,
because finally after decades of schlepping
junk and crap and who knows what
from apartment to apartment,
I had decided to clean house, and
there she was, handsome enough indeed.

∼

I remember her young only once. It was
the middle of my first summer in Schuylerville.
We'd driven to Smith College, my uncle Bob
and I, to visit her for an afternoon.
She was in a graduate program, earning
a degree in psychiatric social work.
The rest of the year she worked for almost nothing
at the Reading D.P.A., trying, I suppose,
to heal in others what never heals.
I was still a haywire kid, maybe nine, so the drive

dragged on, though it took only the morning
to get to Northampton from Schuylerville.
I remember it was a clean, clear, sunny Sunday.
I remember my uncle talking about Dom DiMaggio,
saying he was almost as good as his brother Joe,
while we walked up the hill
from the parked Nash to the dorm house
where she stayed that summer.
I don't remember the name of the house or much else,
except we waited for her inside the front door.
A woman said she was still upstairs in her room,
and went to fetch her. The house seemed dark
but probably wasn't, and the wait wasn't long.
Then she came down the stairs, almost skipping,
dressed like coeds dressed in the late forties—
pleated skirt (light gray?) and brown & white saddle shoes—
and she was glad to see me.
And happy, she was fucking happy.

NOTES

Locations:
Reading, Pennsylvania
Schuylerville, New York
Northampton, Massachusetts
D.P.A. is The Department of Public Assistance

Monday, September 27

I.

I try to imagine that day for her,
all those years ago, those strict times,
legitimacy and the corrections
of shame, man-abandonment, nuns,
their stern compassion, her coming to term
in a distant city, maybe one friend
from college, college a shattered cup. I can't.
Each time I try, the story runs from me.
Hers alone those years never spoken of.
Even on her deathbed not worth much time,
the words between us spare, every-day.
She seemed elsewhere, as if behind a veil.

II.

In my mind, it's always a gray day
but not raining (not that cliché). Cold
in the morning air, early autumn,
the snow-belt of New York getting ready
for the discipline of winter; though
it could have been just as easily
a beautiful day in late September,
the sky an intense, luminous blue, golden
light striking the lake surface, mist rising.
But all that would have happened hours later.
I was born around three in the morning.
Beyond the hospital, a cloudless night,
therefore, the wide white arc of stars.
You could see them then, on any clear night.
They filled the vault, spoke the silence.

III.

Only once did she talk about that day.
It must have been around the time Jack died,
in Seattle, in summer, sick, alone.
Strange, the one missing from all our lives, the one
I'd forget each morning, made present by death.
No one back home knew what his life was like;
how his days spun with alcohol schemes,
nights adrift in terrors, how far from them,
and from me, he was. I was not yet eight.
They wrote each other letters. I think she
thought about him a lot, like a secret.
I didn't. I mean hardly ever except
if someone asked me where my father was.
Then I'd repeat lies my mother told me;
only I didn't know they were lies. They were
my story. People liked hearing me tell it.
I didn't realize that they knew the facts
and were having themselves a bit of fun.

∼

She said I was born with jaundice. My eyes
were yellowed. She said I was Monday's child
and smiled. I doubt she saw the irony
or didn't want to see it. Yet there it was.
I think an innocence had claimed her:
little yellow albatross, soon so torn a spirit.
And the rhyme? We both would know Wednesday's woe.—
No matter. It all came down to that last
hospice visit with death in the corner.
Silence. Curling smoke. The cigarettes seemed
a small *So what!* She got to talking some,
but most of the pieces stayed missing.
Finally, her secret, the few words.

IV.

The hall lights of hospital corridors
are also yellow if you travel back,
the lost time rushing forward to meet you
halfway between now and death's milieu:
again the papers signed, hurried goodbyes,
rushed prep, again the long roll of the gurney,
ceiling lights slipping past, their fans dark wings,
contractions beginning to bunch, the stone
deep in the hips like the weight of the world
tearing through your body, isolation
setting up like ice, the mind gone with fear.
And then the moment the doors swing open,
the sharp change in the light as you enter,
and they are waiting for you, a circle,
to do what they have done a thousand times
and a thousand times before, and before,
what you will do only once in your life,
yoked, as you are, to the consequence.
But now you are the celebrated guest,
your trembling legs are opening again,
the wildness this time all pain and fury.

The Cross You Chose

"After all your mother's done for you!"
her father would spit out, almost shouting,
almost reaching across the dinner table
to smack me (which he never did),
after I'd been harshly disrespectful to her,
again, and as always, her saying nothing back,
perhaps because of some progressive
child-rearing philosophy she subscribed to,
perhaps something else.
I had a sharp tongue, even before
adolescence struck. I never understood why.
It was like a reflex, a quick blade to slice with,
as if in answer to some always near, inchoate threat,
its vagueness like a half-open, angled door, white
hallway, line of evenly spaced, yellowish ceiling lights,
thrumming, maybe a big room full of sick kids bedding down,
my three-year-old self one of them but not sick—
that time before sleep, shadows, and another day
not to be remembered.

$\sim$

I can't say how often the little dinner scene
played out. But there was a last time.
I was twelve or thirteen, strange to myself.
I pushed back, demanded he tell me
what more, exactly, had she done
than mothers are supposed to do.
I was looking him straight in the eye,
expecting to get hit hard. Nothing.
"Never mind," he said, then silence. He had folded
or was trying to spare my mother further pain.
Only I couldn't read him for that. So, the needed words
didn't show up that day nor any day.

I was a difficult kid, not bad, just difficult.
And I was indeed the cross she had chosen to bear
and I had no goddamn idea about any of it.
I just had my "reflex." Over time
I got easier to be around. By senior year
of high school, I was almost
a model student, college bound.
She had managed to tame the surface of me.

REPRISE

Launched! Everything nicely in place.
My bright-and-shiny future arriving.
What would I tell them if I could call
them to this room, the one always out of earshot,
the one never truly free? I made a mess of it.
Would they be honestly surprised?

Freshman year held together despite
the lost feeling. Kept my head down and traded
on my high school goods. Next year fell apart.
Almost before the leaves were down. No reason
I could point to. As if what I had been evaporated
and the residue, the dregs— me from now on.

Sleeping days, chasing sex became the story—
not the having but the hungering
until finally a few misalliances.
Then the lying about feelings, private
shame. A guilt so black I couldn't see the lie
coming back. How bewilderingly alone we were.

And so it went. I climbed aboard the chaos.
And to the rescue? Marriage. Because they hadn't.
Because that's how we'd been brought up
in that stretch of the twentieth century.
And it didn't have a thing to do with love
and everything to do with my parents' story.

THE MIDDLE YEARS

And then she was free, her penance concluded.
No more making sure the boy made it through.
I had reached that point where Jack's life and hers
had unraveled. How unfavorable the odds had been.
But now college, a good school. I was on my way.
And her middle years opened up. They were hers.
The lover could come out of the shadows.
She could invite him to the apartment.
Dinner, drinks, records playing on the hi-fi—
the man could sleep over. Just one life now.

Winter Departure on a Commuter Train Platform, Early Sixties

She might have gotten to the untold story,
the whole of it, not merely given advice
about no more trying for a third child
after my wife's back-to-back miscarriages,
and I would have had to regard the meddling,
instead of keeping faith with silence and
the task at hand, which was repeatedly
to scan the empty length of narrowing track,
as if that could fetch the commuter train
ahead of schedule and get her on her way,
returning us to the distance between us....
She would be decades gone before I knew
I should have stepped into that conversation.

Two Letters, Ten Years Apart

They pretty much despised each other,
my first wife, my mother. It had never
been open warfare. More a strained truce.
So when my mother called and expressed
what seemed to me genuine sympathy,
after Christopher John, six hours in this world,
died, my wife felt the plunge of a cold knife.
I didn't. But for some reason, I wasn't sure.
In the days that followed, my wife campaigned.
How could I not feel my mother's cruelty,
how her words mocked my wife's suffering?
I must write my mother, confront her.
And there it was, my mother or my wife.

∼

We were wrong, of course, but youth-blind
to something complex yet heartfelt,
to words beyond our years. Grief had made us
crazy, in need of a target. So the letter
I should not have written. Then ten years' silence.

∼

December, a second letter.
After so much time, it must have been,
in its sealed envelope, unnerving.
And yet, wasn't this the season of hope,
when the grace of renewal is in the air?

∼

I was one year divorced, my children
lost to me, which is where she'd known
things would end up. So that was the news
I opened with. Then, still lived in the same town,

same job, saw my kids some weekends.
I used a light touch, but finally I got to it:
wrote how sorry I was about the first letter,
said we'd both made our share of mistakes
that were hard to get past, but hoped we could,
closed with something about the season and Christmas.

After the second letter, others followed.
I wrote in the kitchen at a card table,
often a bottle of wine, a lit candle,
the rest of the apartment in darkness.
We had begun working our way through
the damage. Next Christmas, I flew East.
Eleven years. It would be thirty more
before I understood why she had said *yes*.
But the answer, had I asked myself, was
right there, in that child-empty one-bedroom.

December Visit

She had rented a second floor apartment
in one of those rectangular stone houses
you find in the Northeast. This one might have
been built around the time of the Revolution,
the interior modernized a few years back
and nicely appointed. A warmth to the light.

The living room had a large bay window.
Outside, in the yard next door, and taking up
most of the yard and half the view, a copper beech
she had come to cherish, especially in autumn
when the leaves turn bronze-red through late November,
but now bare-branched. She took great care to point it out.

That was the moment the copper beech became the totem.
Of course, neither of us knew it then, nor thought the word.

Missing Chapter

When did I know I needed to learn your life?
It was too late for facts, Eva Mae, and when
did I start to see ghost connections, tangled
resemblances revealed in mirrors, figures
of speech, the odd way I clear my throat, two lives
playing out a parallel of errors?

I thought it was the fiction of my father
I had been assigned to pursue, page by page,
his voice my voice as the first poems broke through;
I thought that way, the way of my redemption,
but how could a young man, alcohol ruined,
redeem? It was just me, an ordinary need.

∼

So much hurt and vehemence in my aunt's voice.
It surprised me. As if you'd never thanked her
for being the rock and glue of your last years.
She wanted me to know what I wouldn't: broken
affairs, late-night drunk dialing, your bitterness…
That was the evening, the day we buried you.

Next day, the first of how many graveside hours,
overdue questions, reliable silence?
One gets on, learns the ignorance, though the need
for the facts of your life is never not felt.
The time of healing lay far beyond the time
that was yours to have. My time stretched long enough.

Autumn, Actually September

The shift in the light, the first chill,
sharpness to the morning air,
jeweled grass, a few leaves down,
that September day would come,
the harmonies of nostalgia
would lift your voice a little,
the words every time
nearly the same, a sentence or two,
soon a trailing-off....

❧

The words had the feel of mystery.
All those Septembers—
I never realized
it was the college years,
my father, the two of you
pulling you back.

❧

September.
Those last days shut away
with the sisters
of dubious mercy,
your body heavy with me,
perhaps a slight reprieve
from the days of summer swelter—
you came to term.
Then the life-long consequence,
although in time the years
would cloak the shame
that never quite let go of us.

Fall Leaves of the Copper Beech

Fall leaves of the copper beech, late flame,
and I think this time I will get down
      to the bone fact
      of the tree itself,
bare branches scoring a winter sky.

~

But the season always turns, tendrils
unfurl, buds bloom… subterfuge in green.
      O spring beguiles,
      the sap is running,
summer leaves to copper ashen bone.

~

Each time only beauty shows itself,
that old ignorance like a blessing
      leafs out till fall,
      curtaining the loss,
those broken lovers November's ghosts.

~

Autumn lyric, time-seasoned sorrow:
there's comfort in this practice; yet fixed
      to winter branch
      a bead of amber,
black speck of life—my father's poem.

Encounter with My Father
—for Jack

I'm too old, Jack,
not to have
forgiven you.
I know something now
of your youth-despair,
the greed of sorrow,
the hunger for women.
It's not as if
I haven't lived
my own version
of your misspent life.
Yet even now
there's a stone
in my heart,
a grievance
that won't lift.
If by some
untoward grace,
you were granted
life again, and if
this time we came
upon each other, two
men in a foreign city,
and recognized
one another,
I'd want to ask
forgiveness for
this entrenched
judgment of
my narrow mind,
and I would lower
my eyes, blue as yours,
as I do now
in the numb silence
in which I stand,

to learn again
how you rest:
line of seven
granite stones marking
a family's progress,
one prodigal below,
one still above,
unforgiven, and
without.

What Called Her to Her Silence

To have told me when I was
a boy the untold story,
the whole of it, meant to hear
every day the word whispered
in the way I said my name,
see it in my curtained eyes—
she could not have borne the years.

HOSPICE

There were
    Two cross-country flights, the nursing home visit
And the hospice visit, you still able
    To manage chain-smoking in bed, into the near perfect
Silence, the words like crumbs scattered on a forest floor,
    Myself with nothing of use to say, thinking
The silence was strength, that I was lending you
    Strength, that sitting by your bed, us not looking
At each other while you lit cigarette after cigarette
    And from time to time slipped a cough drop to sooth your throat,
Sufficed…

Mostly you spent
    The slow minutes studying the ceiling, the curling smoke
As if there were still a few signs to be read—and me?
    I studied my hands, busied my mind with nothing.
But somewhere near the end, the trackless hour broke, and you
    Were saying, *Your father and I never married,*
You know, your voice a small calm, as if the weight
    Need be borne no longer. *But I guess you knew*, you say,
And I say, *Yes, I knew*, and that was it, not one word more
    Of the secret we both had kept for each other, forty years
For the want of love.

Lament in Black

I want to write the poem in which she
overcomes, the poem of long delayed
victory, some rise out of the ashes
of her life. Something before it took her,
made a wraith of her, a bag of terror.
I think I would have to lie. But was there
perhaps a brief time before the cancer
revealed itself, when she shaped life to her
liking: art galleries? a faithful lover?
a faithful friend?… There was a young woman,
a coworker, I'm told she got close to,
whom I met at the funeral. Her name
escapes me. I remember our distance
at the after-burial reception.
Some words, awkward glances, silence mostly.
Wasn't she the daughter my mother should have had?
I remember thinking something like that,
and that she knew things about me even I
didn't know. That her silence might be her bond,
holding safe my mother's secrets. So maybe
something lovely did happen in those last years.

September Nostalgia

—for Eva Mae

Today, I'm remembering you
        remembering your happiness…

II. Dark Sounds and Light, a Progress

"The duende won't appear if he can't see the possibility of death."
—Federico García Lorca

THE LAST OF THE ELM LEAVES

The discipline of that sound dry leaves make under foot
like ruined mercy, as if by sound alone it were settled,
what lives past its life, replying to its life, neither
hearing nor sensing, speaking as it breaks, releasing

the last of itself below the dying elms in August,
bested in time by the rolling in of violent weather,
the great voice hidden in the black roil, the fissuring light,
then the avalanche of rain putting an end to the precise grammar;

so that now, deeper in, soaking begins the rotting,
the brittle flesh yielding to silence and slow heat,
the leaf-carpet thickening along the trails, acrid mash
sticking to the soles, and beneath, a warmth, then earth itself…

this humiliation, like the verses of grief,
of voices lost, not one of us will not know it.

Night Falling

They will come quietly into the room
that last day, singly or paired, like stragglers,
like lost friends or lovers, forgotten kin.
They will meet the distance in the man's eyes
as best they can, then take uneasy leave.
And because the casement window is open,
he might recall the receding clack of shoes
crossing a courtyard in Andalusia
as they return to the wants of their lives.

Finally the evening voices will fade.
No foot-strike on the stone stairs or oak door
slowly opening, that splinter of light
penetrating the room. Instead, the sweet
intense fragrance of jasmine will enter
and the raveling whisper of the fountain,
and now the blue of lapis lazuli tiles,
the elegant symmetries below—all this
will mix with the contents of his drifting mind,

until, high above the water sound,
the call of an owl breaks from the trees
and the night air transforms into a presence.
Memories and the confusion of dreams.
The man will not be sure what time in his life
he is living nor why isolation
has come back. He was hardly different,
except for the name they had marked him with.
And the only answer will be the light leaving.

THE MARK

I think the grave and its stone
is a mark but not the soul's mark.
That's a fleeting thing grief might see

as when I go to the two graves,
my mother's, my father's, encounter
those flat stones, their names, the cold dates.

At each grave, I fold one paper crane.
I make the folds sharp, find the form,
place the small carrier of souls

on its marker, then snap a photo
before the wind finds the slight cargo.
I hope, every time, to see straight through.

Instead, that too familiar silence
and the opacity of grass.

THE MOURNING LIGHT

How blinding the silence
once time was done with them,
and I stood by those graves,
confronted.
        Valley Forge,
Saratoga—they were as
separated in death
as in their lives. Questions
would come. They always did,
like prison guards making
late rounds. But the answers
had gone to ground. Nothing
could free me from the debt,
and yet the mourning light
kept offering.

        Still, who
has not lived in a dark
unbelieving? So black
such light might seem never
to find its tortured way,
the mind like a crazed stone,
an opal's prisoned fire,
edge-locked mosaic, weld
against the mourning light's
invasion, each fissure
pierced and threaded, loosened,
the luminous pressure
building until at last
grief shatters.

Then heart's dust
like glinting phenocrysts:
as if a diamond light
were the true destiny
of sorrow.

> *phenocrysts*—large crystals visible to the unaided eye,
> usually of perfect crystalline shape, found
> in a fine-grained matrix in igneous rocks,
> such as Sierra Nevada granite; in sunlight,
> they glint like diamonds against the light-to-
> medium gray of the granite.

WAKE

Outside, the light of dusk withdraws
as the mourners enter the house, begin
to thread through the several rooms.
Like the others they dissolve
into the rising talk and drunken laughter
that fill the hollows of the house
as they make their rounds like pilgrims
from station to holy station—
friend, family, that brief forgetting—
until the far room calls them back.
A last time the guest of honor, honored:
circle of gray suits, black dresses,
hemmed in by oddly bright flowers,
each observant drawn into a privacy.
And their children, who watch them
from metal chairs arranged in rows
in the low-lit parlor, are listening
as night unfolds, and moving,
moving up the line.

SHELTER

I wanted to shelter
    all the children
    when I was a child,
    the younger ones—
knowing the wound,
    the reddened thorns
    winding an ankle
    in the tall sweet rye—
it made what difference?

LAMB OF GOD

Who takest away the sins of the world.

Outside, a clan of blackbirds
has descended upon a rectangle of winter grass
so green
it should not be winter.

They are busy, staccato talking,
foraging together among
the blades.

At Eastertime,
somewhere white lilies.

In late autumn,
the fields after harvest
burn.

Always there is war
somewhere
the boys are clanning with their kind,
facing others of their kind
across no-man's land:

Where flags unfurl and colors signify.

Braver than ever tougher than ever.

Ever the fields burning with the blood fire,
ever the mud's thick embrace.

O sweet Lamb, is the lifting rain
taking them back?

Is there somewhere for them
tenderness?

WHAT IN MEN IS SILENT

That he is so often afraid.
That he fears women, always.
That every man is his enemy.
That he never stops being a boy.
That he fears nakedness more than death.
That there are words too gentle for his mouth
and scenes too tender for his eyes.
That each disclosure of the self is
the self hiding in its veils.
That violence is his paramour.
That he feels more alone than the rocks.
That he's already dead, and suspects.
That he's been told about love and calls it sex.
That sex terrifies him.
That somewhere there is a place
and somewhere a woman
to make him whole.
That God is the disturbance he takes seriously.
That for his führer, his priest, his master,
his mullah, his sergeant…
he is slave and soldier.
That he's heard the rumor of love,
and his longing shatters him.

Easter Morning Among the Stray

We can pray inside the loss.
We can say a song was heard
in the valley of white stones,
that it tells how beautiful
grieving is as it opens
into the morning of hope,
when the body is risen
again, lifting us, the stray,
who have gathered in this house
once more to seek, with only
our sorrow to guide us home.
We can praise as does water,
as do fire and air and earth,
that which is and is part of.

STALKING THE *DUENDE*

"Seeking the duende … there is neither map nor discipline."
—Federico García Lorca

Yesterday, midafternoon,
I tried to catch sight of the *duende*,
because I am a contrary soul
and believe light should be
no impediment. I took my time.
But there, at my usual table
near the front window, November
light reaching into the café,
the moment seemed no more
than a flake of ash. Never mind
we weren't cloaked in the usual darkness.
It had to be there,
in the flickering half-images
at the edge of the eye.

Perhaps it wanted me to work harder.
So I started with the thread of light
that limned the shoulders
of my café mates, meticulously
tracing each filament. But I soon saw
I was seeing only what was behind them
and then the street scene beyond
the café's glass. I looked away,
thinking the outside was too optimistic
for a prey as dark as mine.
I even looked over my shoulder. Nothing.
Then I looked inside myself, which is where
I believed it had been spotted last.
It seemed as well not there.

Is it I have lost the rich scent of freshly-turned, damp earth,
have yet to see the blood-red moon on All Hallows' Eve, or
my faux insouciance as I pass the graves— makes me blind?

AMERICAN ROOTLESS

Once I stood by her stone, in the faithful silence
of her rest near Valley Forge, where the East
offers the best of itself: lush sward of grass,
well-groomed graves sloping toward the creek
hidden behind a line of hardwoods, the daily
gathering of waddling geese tending the grounds—
        fixed in a downpour
that seemed Old Testament in its intentions.
I don't remember exactly when it was, how
far into the past one must travel to retrieve
that aimless son, but nearer the hour winter earth
received the coffined body, sky the slate-gray
of sullen February.
              I sensed a great intention
had found me, and I was glad at first to be
discovered. My heart lifted. Then the storm took aim,
drenching the grass, turning the air a grayish pearl,
into which dissolved granite monuments, trees,
hunkered down geese, the nearby graves.
Yet I gave myself to it, to the hard memories
it demanded. Sorrow got a hold. For a while,
I held my ground.
           A last time by the grave,
a last sheltering in the car, the rain like lead shot
striking metal. Relentless clanging. A small terror,
the need to run—
        West! Pennsylvania farms speeding past,
shining in the glaze-light, the car seeming to fly:
curving climbs, worn mountains, the long descent.
The rain began to lift near Pittsburgh,
      dark by the Ohio line.

                 ❧

Memory: what must be so or hides in its own stories or
is lost in the dissolving light of late afternoon, and me
driving the interstates, nonstop, seeking a thousand miles
of somewhere else, running like freight through the sweet black of night—
Pennsylvania, Ohio, Indiana, the eastern edge
of Illinois, and twenty miles southwest of Chicago
dawn unsealing the night and the early light revealing
a changed land, flat and still and wide, the stubble browns of harvest
overtaking the fields, tractor-turned earth and fallow earth:

To say I have driven the interstates at night too often,
to say I have fallen in love with the motion of night,
to say lights approach and quickly pass and narrow to nothing,
to say one is so perfectly alone one can't be lonely,
is to say love cannot hide forever inside the darkness.

Winter Bird & the *Bruja*

The man would have the blessing were he to wake.
The angel would bathe him in a blue fire,

but he has lived deep in the dream of winter;
a white stillness took hold, beauty was there.

The cold was almost a soft warmth—
why leave the place of settled things?

Even the raven, fence-perched, didn't move.

                  ~

"Something,"
        the woman of fortunes
tells the man,
         "will disturb the child
            who dreams your life.

"Perhaps a thorn
        jammed under a fingernail
or finally, exhaustion.

"A blue hand will sweep
across your winter sleep—
        quilted night in freefall.

"You will shatter
        into a thousand pieces
among which will be
        the *self* you seek."

April Sonnets

As for the cruelties of April as for loss

A lover teaches with just the shoulder's turn

It happens before it happens it keeps happening

And the shadow of love becomes the form of love

And you descend your future arrives

The usual dark the winning dark the spinning dark

Scent of stale beer mildew & memory

The zig-zag way of things

You are a soliloquy of recycled words

Many are redacted others won't leave

Doesn't everyone want a say

There's the unseemly business of *mea culpa*

And the frantic search for footnotes

Where the truth lies

∾

As for the urgencies of April

As for the formless time the yield of years

As for the female light

In the April dusk bearded irises in a yard

Yellow and purple veils hanging in still air

And leaves a thicket of green swords

A path two walking side by side

Old and new raveling before them

Knowing not to look that sideways look

Knowing not yet to touch

And they sense the sweet danger rising

The brush of zephyr on lips

And their words their bodies await them

Only steps from here

The Copper Beech

—for Chris

Mother's Day, the tree leafed out,
full foliage. On the ground, shifting
leaf-shadow, azure overhead.
In late May the leaves tend coppery-green;
in autumn they linger, the last to flame,
as my mother would say.

I have come here often over the years,
alone, to remember my mother, who
gave me art, the faith of introspection,
who taught me the beauty of the copper beech.
I never thought I'd share this place.
But unaccountably a woman
has come into the last season.

We are circling, slow pace, touching
the broad trunk, looking up as we go;
above branches seem to spin:
a spiral turning of spokes, filtered light,
the hub narrowing into the upper reaches.

I think I've healed some, I say.
She seems not to hear me as we follow
the curving trunk. She's fallen easily
into this walking ritual, my private Mass,
like one who's known contrition's prayer.

This beech is true, I say, as committed
to the rites of the Earth
as an elephant matriarch.
And we stop circling. And we say,
how thick the trunk, how far
the heavy branches near the ground run.
I say, cantilevered;
she says, half-zagging horizontals.

And she asks me to believe
they could extend almost to the ends of the earth,
never touching leaf-fall or gravel.
Of course, I say, look how perfectly
the under-arcs have scored the trunk
where the branches form the join,
and we agree the bark is an elephant gray—

yet it leaps, we say,
with a swift unweighting,
like a great dancer,
the higher branches soaring straight up,
converging, as if spirit,
not matter, comprised them, their leaves
thirsting, like the fingertips of the soul…

I call her the summer of my mind.

KNOTTED LOVE STORIES

There was her husband's death
a few years after she came back.
For a long while it was the shadow
that lived inside our life.
And there was the time between,
when she'd left, to honor
the promise that held for them
no future, the year of clandestine
phone calls, her voice the sound
of distance and hollow rooms.

～

Or told another way,
we were outlaw lovers,
it seemed a day. Then she was gone,
back to the life before ours,
and I descended into
the habit of my darkness.
But it came right, the years.
As for the *duende*,
I do not know if it lurks
in the shadows or is the shadow.

A Cosmology

—for Chris

The night goes on forever,
but there are pockets in it,
here and there. They come and go.
They're not always bursts of light.
Sometimes they're just holes in God,
which is what makes everything
problematic. With that kind
of topology, who can
tell the situation we'll
find for ourselves at bottom?
Wasn't it better when it was
Great Turtles all the way down,
or better when love and soul
and such words seemed real enough
to take us through the darkness?
No, Chris, I don't like endless
night, don't like the holes in God.
But all in all, you love me—
more than good enough for dust.

THE HOUR

In the later afternoon, I could see evening
coming so clearly, it seemed arrived already.
Then evening, as if itself the seal of night.

Morning was just morning, and even noon was,
despite talk of the coming heat, still noon.
But afternoon broke and time fell out of time.

∼

One needs something lost returned. Not innocence,
not ignorance, but a fall into that moment
when mind seemed fit to everything the day offered,

the time so wide it was like a promise to the soul.
But now the last Angelus. The dog wants its walk.
So simple the hour that took all the day to find.

Jay Schobber's Evening Prayer, His Country Home

Thou art the dusk light of summer
in eastern Pennsylvania,
the war a worn ghost. Thou art these
children playing their game of tag
on the broad lawn, so cool the air.
Thou art my eyes as wild you run
from hiding place to hiding place,
not hearing the slow labor
of my breathing, the fading beats,
the quiet talk of friends. Thou art
that child of words, evening-veiled,
I won't know, not man nor poem
in three-score and five. Thou art the dance,
the August fireflies' flickered light.
Thou art the delight of children.

III. This Mind That Thinks and Thinks It Is Not Dust

"For dust thou art, and unto dust shalt thou return."
—*Genesis* 3:19 *KJV*

Mortality Ode

Because I was not always conscious,
because I formed between fetus-fish and first grader,
because I was taught my face in a mirror,
because my mother taught me my pronoun and the name
        belovèd and placed her words in me,
because energy moves in and out of forms, heightening
        and lowering the configurations,
because I cannot remember my birth, cannot remember my
        first reflection, cannot remember my first word, nor
        the first time I saw my mother, nor her heartbeat from
        within her, nor her milk-filled breast,
because flames are struck, flare, fade, fail,
because flames ride the nothingness,
because I eat inert life every day but never the spirit flame
        no longer residing there,
because flames passing into flames save nothing of themselves,
because mind is a made thing and the poet's sleep of forgetting
        is neither sleep nor forgetting,
because this consciousness rises from the wick of my body,
because my dead mother will not visit me,
because my dead father will not visit me, nor my dead son,
        nor again the ghost of the friend I betrayed,
because I am merely human
        but cannot find forgiveness there,
because my soul is the unseen house guest, the great rumor
        of the stair,
because God will not talk to me,—
        I know I die.

Praise Dust

Praise the dust that swirls in the dry field
And the dust that weaves an arabesque of insect-light,
Signaling summer's life in evening air,
Praise the dust hungering for us, that does not forget,
That rests on the leaves and drifts and burrows the pistil,
And praise the dust that was the firmament
When the firmament began, and praise
The disturbances of dust
That transmute it
Out of itself and into itself,
Praise the ceaseless anarchy of the small invisible
And the calling of dust into stars
And the calling of stars into wheeling islands
And the islands into archipelagoes of light,
And praise the light that emanates and spans,
Threading the blackness, praise
The countervailing blackness separating
Island and star from island and star,
And praise the dark matter's containing
That holds true the star wheel,
Praise the centrifugal uncertainty,
Yet praise the planet's forming in the sun's circle,
In the spinning dust,
Praise this blue home buried in the star wilderness,
Praise volcano and mountain, desert and sea,
The roiling interior and spinning iron
And the field of lines that turns away
The solar stream of death,
Praise the many-hued skin of air, how it sponsors
The light fall that showers ocean and land,
And the luminous clouds and the gray, rain-filled clouds,
The shearing, zagging light, the clap of thunder,
Praise the scum that became life,
Praise the clay that became life,
Praise the waters of life and the carrying wind,

Praise fire, ignitor of all things,
And praise with abiding grief the proposition of death,
How that which flees from itself in terror and blindness yet yields
That itself may live,
Praise what I eat, what eats me,
And praise I will become the dust of my name
And my name the dust,
Praise that we lived, you and I,
Praise the singular moment of our being,
Praise love's late season, our life together,
Praise the loves we have known,
Praise the trees and the hands of the trees,
Praise equation
And number, poem and song,
Praise how time will bring the sun closer,
How the water and air will boil away
And the spreading desert will inherit
The continents, the floors of the sea, praise the wind
That before it dies will lift aloft
All that lived and will in its dying let down
In dust the last rain of earth,
And praise the wind of the sun that shall give up the earth
To the void and the explosion of stars
And the star's rekindling,
Praise this mind that thinks
And thinks it is not dust,
Praise us, soul-demented beings of ruin,
Praise chance, praise words, praise love,
And praise the dust swirling the field this very moment.

IV. A FEW REMARKS IN PASSING—*JISEI* POEMS

my life
came like dew,
disappears like dew—
all of Naniwa
is dream after dream.
—Toyotomi Hideyoshi
(1536 – 1598)

Note: In Japan, *jisei* is a type of poem that meditates
on death and mortality, often coupled with
observations on life; a poet's farewell poem
to life, usually neither grim nor morbid.

Gladness and Grace

More than a decade now
since writing the first *jisei*,
but when you're a survivor
each day is the perfect
occasion for writing
the next poem, for finding
in the small, the large,
in this one season, four.

At Coupa Café

It began with death moods.
I would come here afternoons,
after radiation, like a secret,
for coffee and notebook-musings.

I believed doom, felt
myself the borrowed hours,
certain how the hand plays out,
time the only wild card.

But melancholy
would soon give way. I would write
anew love poems to this café world.
Had I landed in my life?

Calling

When I was young,
I followed so
many false dreams.
To be a great poet
was one of them,
which was to be,
I think, my father,
which is funny
or silly or sad,
because in truth
he was nothing
but a rumor
my mother spun
when I asked
for some angled
secret of my own
I could keep close
while I ran the streets
with the boys
who went home
to fathers.

The Last Decaders

Seasoned grief, gain
long age allows,
boon and new grace—
the young can have
no use for us
as they busy
rush toward where
we were by then.

Scenes of My Lived Life

These days scenes of my lived life
      keep coming through.
It's a common ailment of my years.
Nothing grandiose or boisterous,
      little of regret.
Instead what comes and goes
like quanta of the briefest time leaves
      a sweet after-image:
a moment, a figure, the angle of light
      are present-changed,
      yet recognition—
as if my life were signaling my life.

Aubade

You and I, we move
through our night of shadows
almost easily now—
alone, we think, the witness
of our passion as self-hidden
as Pacific cypress
weathering in coastal fog—
as when deep in the roil
of lust and doubt,
we took our leave of love
before the morning light
broke in.

JISEI FOR THE LAST DECADERS

Drop by drop
they rise from
the green blades
     silently
     into air
that's silver
winter mist
and no one's
     the wiser
for the dreams
that once cast
their shadows
     like faces.

THE PLAY OF TIME

As if a threadbare curtain dissolves
and scenes of before play out again,
as if young people, dead now or soon,
are moving through an unmeasured time....
They don't see me here (I don't see me),
but once more we get on with the blind
business of our lives, repeating lines,
the scripted gestures, the search for love.
Something always breaks, yet I am glad
for the reprise. The year is turning.

It Comes Back to Me

Polished bone & river silt,
black mud at the weedy edge
of storied waters, oozing
thick between my toes
as I waded in, half-fearful
of something I couldn't name
the summer my voice changed.

UNBIDDEN

If it weren't they disappear
about as fast as they appear,
they'd pile up and leave
no room for the future.

They always surprise
the ordinary hours,
make it worth my while
to attend the matinee.

There's never a madeleine
involved or its after-clue
of crumbs trailing into
the requisite dark wood.

And besides, they're benign or
at their worst they mildly break
the heart with a newfound loss
of what I didn't know I loved.

Progress

You are caught in your time,
the language at the edge
of your knowledge. It makes
you impatient with what
seems old ground, old voices,
the manner of our words.
It was the same for me.

Ear Training

The whiskery cells are keen
to announce their noisy decline.
I've begun to listen for it,
that woofy hissing in aged ears.
Perhaps some strategic message
requires decoding. Should I
construe the sound of the Universe
is coming through, or is this just
another case of poet's ear?

Instrument

The twilight poet seeks a metaphor
for himself. The usual suspects offer
their service. But it's the Japanese flute
comes to his mind, and how the hollow wood
requires a long, slow breath to raise the notes—

> dark brown cattails moving in river wind,
> a lowering sun glinting yellow-orange
> across the marsh, new bones settling in muck…

He's of an age. That sort of image
from time to time. But then, a smile.

How It All Turned Out Before It Turned a Last Time Bad

Well. It turned out well (don't ask me why).
The *I* I knew improved markedly (don't ask me the odds).
Death got put in its proper place (don't ask me how).
"I'll tarry in the wings a while," it said (don't ask me when).
My mind got free of itself (don't ask me the way).
And settled into the day at hand (amen).

SONNET FOR A SMALL FORGOTTEN CHILD

My life is blessed now, yet unease—
as if something were still undone,
as if a small forgotten child
left roadside a lifetime ago
had stirred and were calling to me
across the dust of eighty years.
I know him, know his injury,
the long grief of those closed-in hours,
how it found its way to poems
he never imagined writing,
his soul the melancholy there.
He's the first-maker and the last,
but there's no time in which he knows
the words. Such a hard equation.

Estate

Hardwood glade,
October's leaf-fall,
that given place

among the colors—
shade, stone,
the dark surround…

let poems
come and go
like fall birds

for anyone
who has still
some need of me.

Penumbral Air: Call & Response

Bones settle, ash swirls,
dry snow drifts across the graves—
    the mind wandering.

But a sudden light breaks in
and the room yields what was lost.

And seen, is returned
as soon to loss—winter bird
    flying into night.

In the growing distance cries
measure the penumbral air.

A deepening gray
quiets the neighboring trees—
    the birds disappear.

Do not despair, friend. Come dawn
they will raise up their ruckus.

THE COMING TIME
—for my daughter and my son

I wonder if you will seek me out
as I did my mother and father
when I needed those two graves to break
their silence and speak unspoken words.

I wonder if one by one you will
arrive at this defeat, as I did,
time and again, learning only loss,
for by then it will be the lesson.

Still, that won't stop you from going there,
won't stop your ear from the hard silence
even though words you have yet to know
you need are for the living to speak.

September Notes

Ah, sad *sabi-san*
of the mirror—you're as vain
    as a peacock's fan.

There's heart,
    there's home, the last
        of this narrow road.

Old man, your shadow
life is shadowing you—
    a kind of light.

The dreamer sleeps
while the moon-summoned dew
    readies the morning grass.

Gathering leaves
as the wind rises—
    September harvest.

…somehow
    something
        then nothing…

Autumn

The Japanese maples
have begun their fall journey—
scarlet will take them, then
curled leaf-edges, rusting.
I am not yet in the ground.

A Few Remarks in Passing

—for my wife

The great tigers,
they are no more.
Even their shadows
drown in shadows.
What would be risked,
dreaming the far wilds,
the love-fever's heat?
Foolish madness, is it
wrong to miss you?

∾

No secret: some go grief-mad
when they hear the grave calling.
And no secret: the glass
that darkens, darkens me.
Yet the light is thee, my love.

∾

Priests can intone, arrange a circle of stones
as in the past, invoke the sacred practice,
or one's friends can assemble in dusk light,
to give voice to prayer—it will help some,
but in the end, love, mad grief is the physician.

∾

If as the Bardos teach, the soul
can't move on while the living
madly grieve, I'd ask for you
to quiet your grieving a while
so I may leave; and I'd pray also
your grief becomes a calm, abiding love.

Self's Journey

From a single point
outward to the edge
of lightless nothing—

it remembers the child
and perhaps in its recesses
the seed, and remembers

the cast shadows of longing
and all that happened to love;
it grew smaller & smaller

and small, so that the world
grew large again, but it has still
itself, the blessing's last.

THE STONE HOUSE

The past swings out in front,
loops back around, closes

Like a circumference wall,
sealing me in a stone house.

I could take torchlight
to deep interiors—

Nothing in the shadows
would have the future in it.

Teach Us to Care

I often imagined the reveries of age
In those years when I knew life would be short and torn,
Allowed myself the pleasures of recollection—
That tangle of scented hair, lustrous in fire light,
Slow staccato of burning logs, the soundless ash,
Silence where words had been, glistening of dark eyes,
Departure. It's what youth knew of what it didn't know,
Though I never thought then I would choose solitude.
And yet life. An old life. A healthy life. My self
Still the flickering illusion, the question mark.
But all around me, the miracle of being,
The "I am" of everything, the loud silence of it,
Which is the quiet inside a poem, when words
Align in the innocence, when an old hand gathers.

[haiku]

Snowmelt, wind-whipped flags,
that crystalline winter light—
must be time to go.

Acknowledgments

2018 Yeats Poetry Prize, Honorable Mention
"Praise Dust"

2013 Montreal Poetry Prize, Long List Anthology
"The Last of the Elm Leaves"

The Sand Hill Review, 2001
"The Copper Beech"

J. David Cummings worked as a theoretical physicist at the Lawrence Livermore National Laboratory for more than ten years. Some years later, after visiting the Hiroshima Memorial Peace Park, he began writing the poems that culminated in his book, *Tancho*, which Alicia Ostriker chose to win the Ashland Poetry Press Richard Snyder Publication Prize in 2013.

His long poem, "Praise Dust" was one of five selected for honors by the W. B. Yeats Society of New York in its 2018 annual competition. Judge Leslie McGrath said of the poem that it "...conjures out of lush sounds the smallness of the self when backgrounded by eternity."

His poems, whether interrogating the world-historical event of the atomic bombings and their long aftermath, delving deeply into the mysteries of human psychology (sometimes with metaphors stolen from physics), or re-membering his own complex and difficult family history, are heart-centered, searingly honest, and layered with multiple meanings. He believes poems must have music, passion, and beauty, and strives to imbue his work with those qualities.

He lives in Menlo Park, California with his wife Christine and a house full of books.